Beach Hemp Jewelry:
Learn the Art of Making Beautiful Braids, Knots, Twists, and Macramé
By: Sara Self

© 2017
Sara Self
Beach Hemp Jewelry

Dedication

Dedicated to my mom who taught me at an early age to enjoy the art of crafting. She has always been my inspiration for learning and trying new ideas. Thank you, mom, for my sewing machine, my craft boxes, my crayons, and most importantly for being my mom.

Also dedicated to my Dad, late Grandmother, and late Papa. They always let me run my craft stores and make my silly drawings when I was little. They would give me nickels, dimes, and quarters for my "products". They even bought my imaginary cheeseburgers from my drive-thru window at my Playhouse Restaurant. Thanks to them the entrepreneur spirit has never left me.

To my friends and family who have bought my jewelry and/or worn my jewelry in the past, thank you for showing me that I can do whatever I put my mind too. Finally, to my best friend and significant other, Jeff who has shown me that I can do anything that I am passionate about.

.

Have you ever thought about making your own beautiful hand-crafted jewelry pieces at home? Ever wonder how to make those twisted knots? Or perhaps how to braids with four strings? This book will show you how. With step by step guide and pictures illustrating the knots I use to make hemp jewelry, I want to make easy for you to learn to make your own.

Table of Contents

Chapter 1: Getting Started - Supplies, Measuring, Creating the Loop and Making Your First Knot

Jewelry crafting is an art that has been around since the stone age. Whether you are looking for a new way to make jewelry or this is your first-time crafting, I would like to share with you how I make beautiful homespun hemp jewelry anklets, bracelets, and necklaces. Let's get started.

First you will want to gather all of your supplies. This may vary a bit depending on if you want to make your jewelry with beads or not. You will however need hemp or hemp cord. Choose the color you like. 100% all-natural hemp is usually a tan or brown color. Hemp cord will be your dyed colors like black, red, green etc. Both make beautiful jewelry. You will also need scissors and a tape measure. You can find all of this on Amazon.com or a local store in the craft department. You may already have it laying around your house.

Supplies needed for hemp jewelry making.

It's time to decide what you are going to make. This way you can measure out your hemp string accordingly. For me it's important not to waste the hemp. I like to measure as exact as possible so that when you finish all of your strings are even.

All ends are close to even, no hemp is wasted.

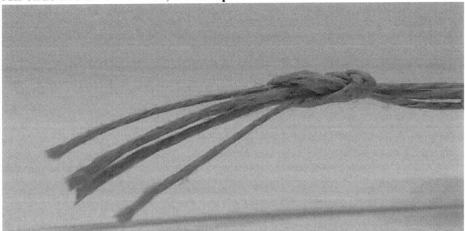

Chapter 1: Continued - Getting Started - Supplies, measuring, creating the loop, and making your first knot

Handmade jewelry, is well, handmade, and will never be exact. Decide if you want a hemp anklet, bracelet, or necklace. Measure with a tape measure (If you don't have one, you can print one out online) your wrist, anklet, or neck length. Then you need to decide if you want your piece to be adjustable too, meaning you can make it tighter or looser. When I measure my own pieces, I usually make them adjustable up to an extra four inches. You will want to figure in those inches when you make this first measurement.

For example: I want to make a hemp anklet. I discover that my ankle is eight inches wide. And I want to leave four extra inches for adjustability. Eight plus four is twelve. But wait we have to figure in the start knot and finish knot too. Otherwise you don't account for the hemp needed to fasten your jewelry together and it would just fall off of you or be too short. Either way, we don't want that happening. Now add another four inches to account for your fastening knots. Twelve plus four, we are at sixteen inches. Great, but you are still not done measuring your first hemp string, yet. The type of jewelry I am going to show you always uses four strings (strands) of hemp. That is two cut pieces folded over. Let's take that number sixteen and double it, that is thirty-two inches long.

Measure out how long you need, be sure to include extra for fastening your jewelry.

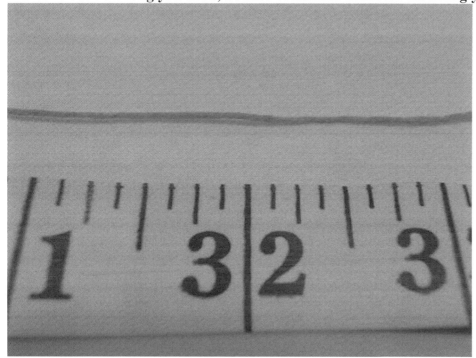

Chapter 1: Continued - Getting Started - Supplies, measuring, creating the loop, and making your first knot

Cut the hemp string at thirty-two inches. We now have our short string.

Cutting the short string after I have measured it.

When you are knotting there will always be one really long string and one really short string when you first measure them out. To make your long string you measure it against the short string not your tape measure. The longer you want your jewelry piece to be the longer this next cut will be. There is no exact formula for this either. However, I have found using this general rule of thumb ends up with the least amount of hemp string wasted. For an anklet you want your long string to be 2.5 x the length of the short string. For bracelets go a bit shorter. And for necklaces I usually measure 4-5 x depending on how long the necklace is. It is best to measure too long and have extra hemp at the end than to measure too short and have to start over.

Measuring the long string from the short string.

Now that you have your short string and long string all measured and cut, it is time to make that first knot. Take your short string of hemp. Fold it exactly in half and make a loop like this.

Folding your short string in half and making a loop.

Chapter 1: Continued - Getting Started - Supplies, measuring, creating the loop, and making your first knot

Now do the same with your long sting of hemp, fold it over in the middle making a loop. Gather your two strings together.

Both the short and long strings are folded over here.

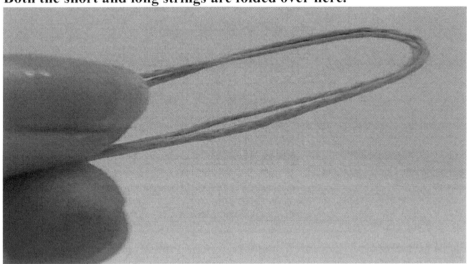

We want to make an over hand knot to tie all the strings together. It's important though to not pull the knot all the way.

Overhand Knot - Step One

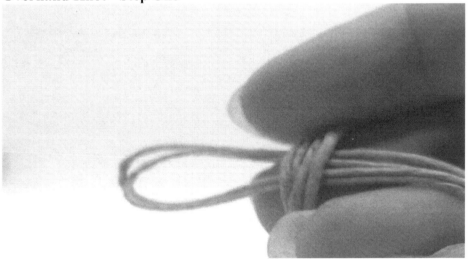

Chapter 1: Continued - Getting Started - Supplies, measuring, creating the loop, and making your first knot

Overhand Knot - Step Two

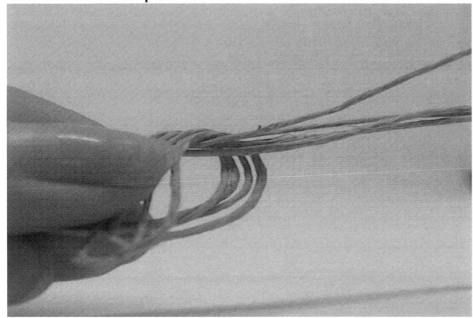

Step 3 Overhand Knot

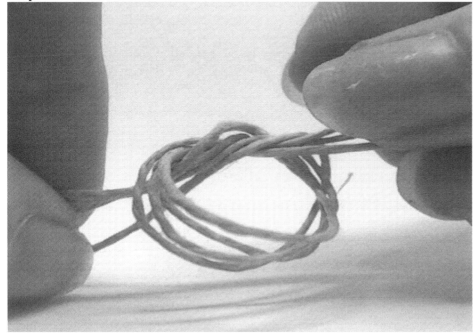

Chapter 1: Continued - Getting Started - Supplies, measuring, creating the loop, and making your first knot

You want to leave a small hole. Use your fingers like in the picture below to make a loop big enough that a knot can go through it.

Making the Loop - Step One

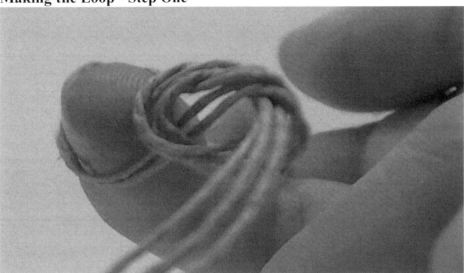

Making the Loop - Step Two

Making the Loop - Step Three

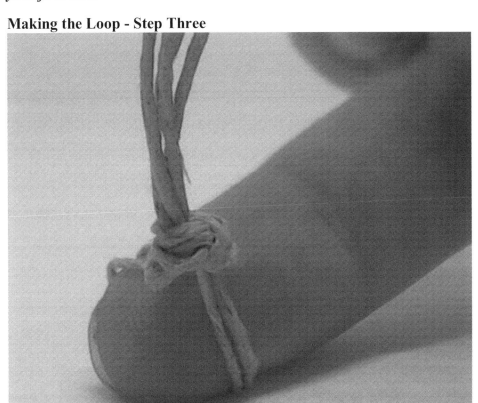

You now have made your first knot, congratulations. Let's move on to some more knots that will add patterns to your jewelry.

Chapter 2: Simple Square Knotting - How to make the square macramé knot and place a bead

Now that you have your starter knot, your jewelry project can go in any direction. The sky is the limit. I want to teach you a few simple knots and you can let the creativity flow from there. A simple square knot is where we will start.

You will want to separate your hemp strings. In order from left to right you should have long string, short string, short string, long string. Those are your four strings and those are what we are going to be using to make our knots.

To make the square knot. Start with right long string. Make a loop over the two short strings in the middle like the following picture.

Looping the right long string over the two middle short strings.

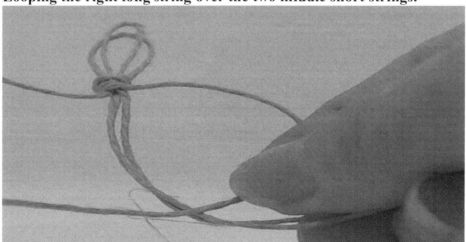

Chapter 2: Continued - Simple Square Knotting - How to make the square macramé knot and place a bead

Now take your left long string and loop it over the right long string.

Looping the left long string over the right long string.

Now use an over and under technique, like when you learned to tie your shoes. The left long string is going over the right long string and under all of the strings. You want to pull the left long string thought the big loop on the right.

Pulling the left long string through the loop.

Pull tight.

Now to get the square pattern you want to repeat with the left side.

Looping the left long string over the right long string.

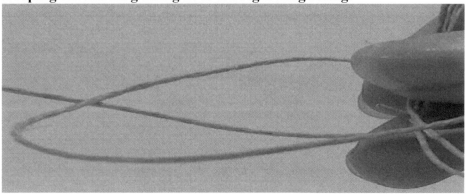

Pulling the right long string over then under.

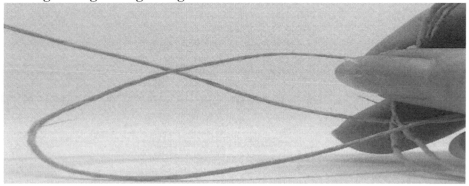

Pull the right long string through that big loop.

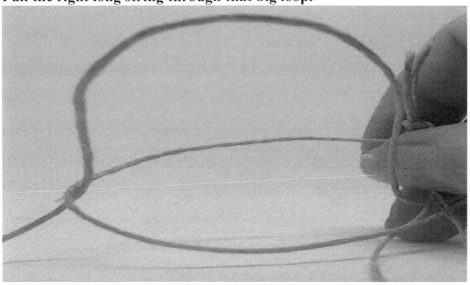

Pull the strings tight.

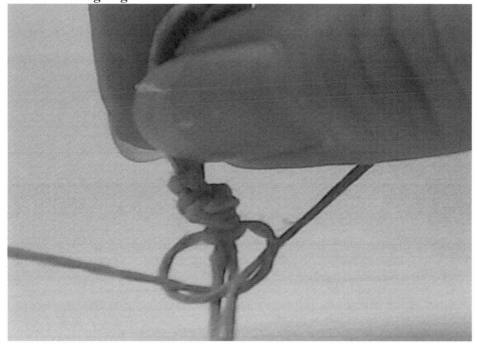

You have now learned how to do the square knot. To finish your piece, continue alternating right string, left string. After a bit your hemp jewelry should start to take form.

Chapter 2: Continued - Simple Square Knotting - How to make the square macramé knot and place a bead

After a few square knots.

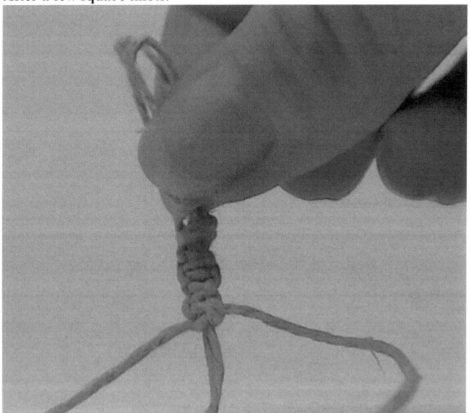

You do not have to put a bead on our piece but you might like too. You can purchase beads at your local crafts stores, department stores or on Amazon. There are also many ways to make beads out of recycled materials. If you would like a bead placed on your piece, string it on the middle strings to have your bead look woven into your jewelry. Or you might want to have your bead look like it is hanging from your jewelry. In this case you would place the bead on one of your longer strings and do the same process. It is up to you.

Decide what kind of bead you want (make sure your hemp fits the bead!)

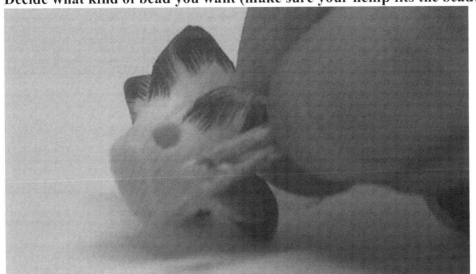

String on your bead (This is with the bead woven into the jewelry look, the bead is thread onto the middle short strings.)

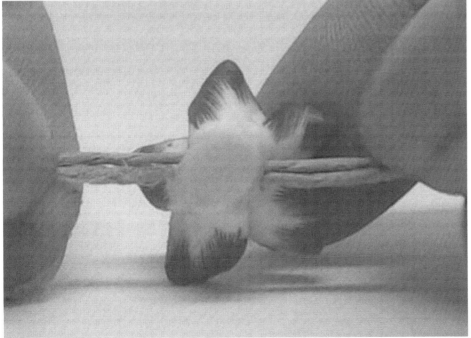

And then make a square knot up under the bead to hold the bead in place. To place a square knot under or after the bead, you just repeat the steps for making a square knot. The next few pictures illustrate how to do this.

Securing the bead with a right tight square knot. Loop the right long string over the middle strings.

Looping the left long string over the right long string and under, then pulling it through.

Chapter 2: Continued - Simple Square Knotting - How to make the square macramé knot and place a bead

Be sure to always pull your knots tight when securing your beads.

Now the bead is woven into your jewelry piece.

This is how the bead would look from the back side. Yours should be similar in tightness.

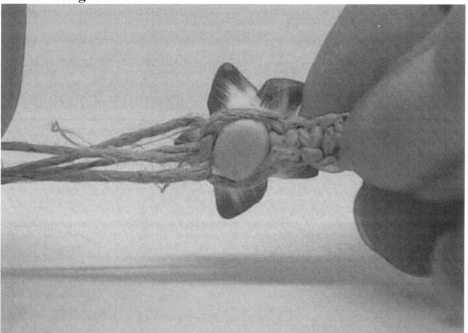

To finish your jewelry piece, you make another overhand knot.

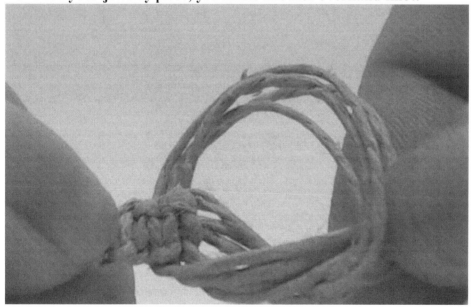

Then you decide how many inches your piece will be adjustable.

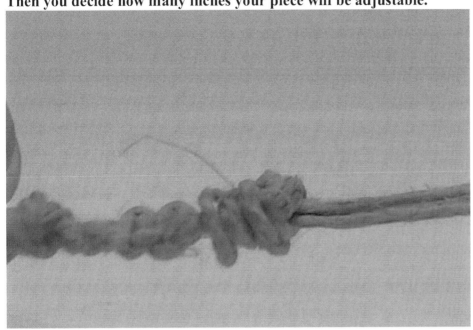

Now make a final overhand knot to finish the jewelry piece.

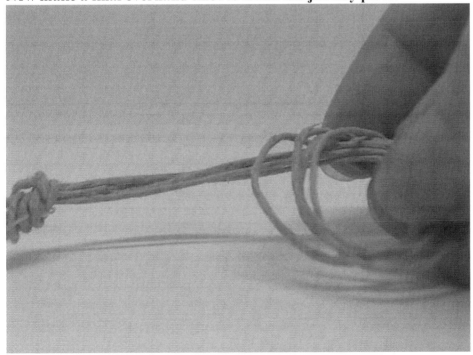

Chapter 2: Continued - Simple Square Knotting - How to make the square macramé knot and place a bead

Cut off any extra hemp strings.

Now let's take a look at the finished product. Looking good there but are you wondering how you will fasten it on? Let's find out.

Slide the strings through the loop you made at the beginning.

Make another overhand knot at the length that you want.

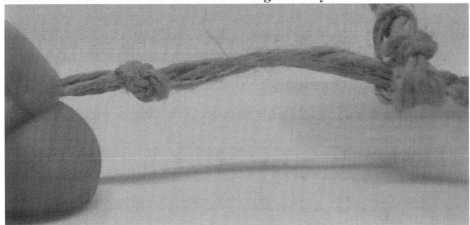

Your jewelry is now secure and you just finished your first hemp jewelry piece. Continue on to the next chapter to learn a different version of this knot that adds character to your hemp jewelry.

Chapter 3: Loose Square Knotting – Adding character to your square knots with loose knots

Ever wonder how those fancy complicated looking knots are made? Fancy is just another word for different really. There are only so many knots in the world. So how can you make your knots different? Loose knotting is one way I have found.

Loose knotting is simply what it means, not pulling your knots tight all the way. You can make your knots as wide or as loose as you want. Adding this technique to your knotting skills increases the different combinations that you can put together. Let's get started.

Making your first loose square knot. I assume you have read the previous chapters before this one. You will need to start with your measured strings, two pieces fold in half. Remember the overhand knot from chapter one that you use to start each jewelry piece? Make that overhand knot and leave room for your loop to fasten your jewelry when you are finished.

Now we are going to repeat the square knot technique from chapter two.

Loop your right long string over the short middle strings.

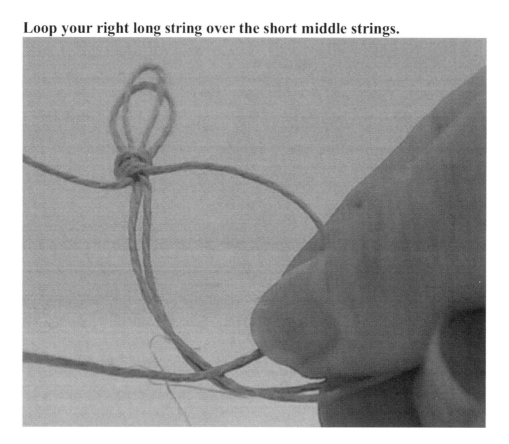

Chapter 3: Continued - Loose Square Knotting - Adding character to your square knots with loose knots

Your left long string then comes under the right string and through the loop.

Pull it though, but this time not so tight!

You can decide how loose to make your square knot. Now repeat with the left side.

Loop the left long string over the middle short strings.

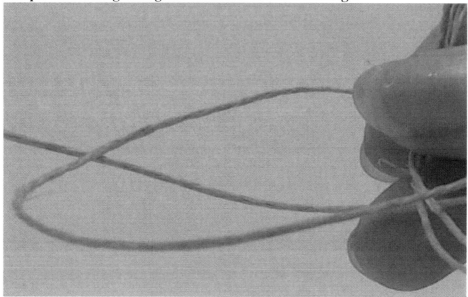

Chapter 3: Continued - Loose Square Knotting - Adding character to your square knots with loose knots

Now place the right long string over the left string.

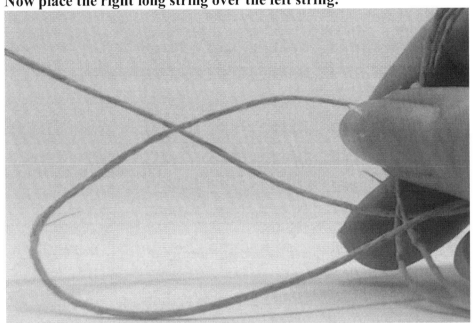

You want to go over it and then under the loop and pull it through.

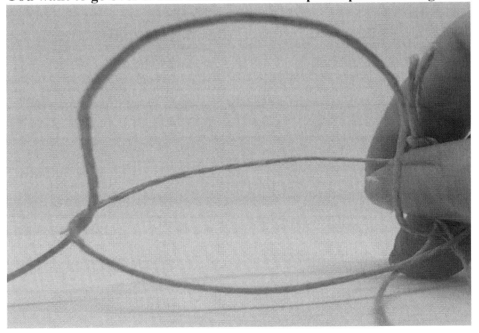

Decide how tight you want this knot to be.

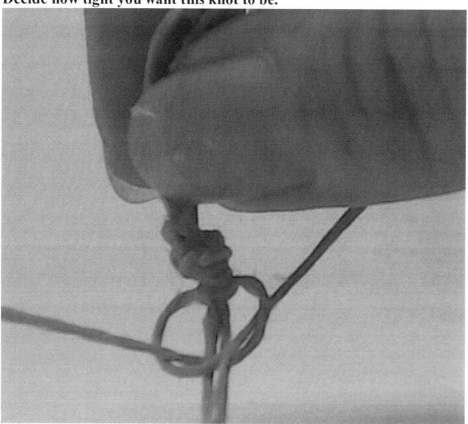

That is two loose square knots.

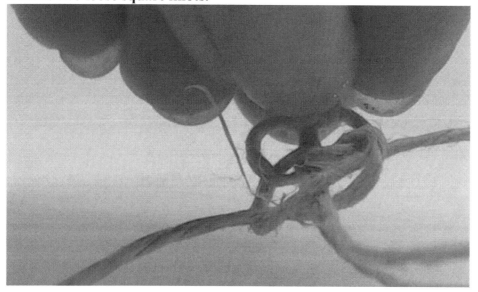

Chapter 3: Continued - Loose Square Knotting - Adding character to your square knots with loose knots

You could make a whole necklace or bracelet out of loose knots or you might want to alternate between loose square knots and tight square knots. It is up to you. You get to be the creator of your jewelry. If you would like to add a bead to your loose square knot jewelry, you can do that. However, you have to use tight square knots, the kind of knot I introduce in chapter two to hold your beads in place. If you want to make a jewelry piece with all or mostly loose knot, you would just make a couple of tight knots when you get close to placing the bead. Then place the bead on the string, secure the bead with a tight knot, and then add a couple tighter knots to make sure the bead is held in place.

To finish your loose square knot jewelry piece, you have to use tight knots. Tight knots will hold your jewelry in place and allow you to be able to fasten it. Make a couple of tight square knots at the end of your jewelry pieces to hold your loose knots in place or overhand knots will work too.

An overhand knot to tie off your jewelry piece.

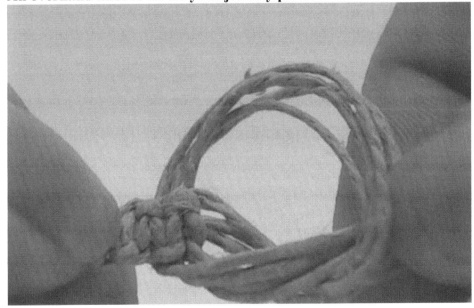

Leave space for how much adjusting room you want.

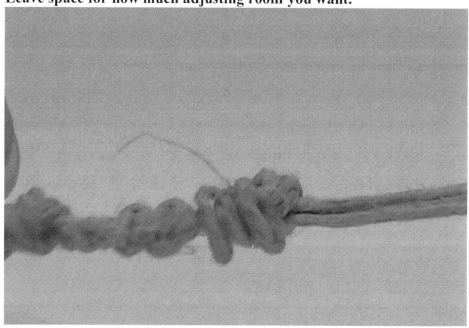

Make another overhand knot.

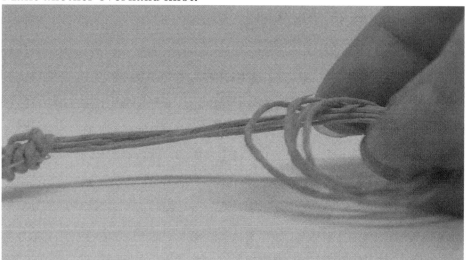

Chapter 3: Continued - Loose Square Knotting - Adding character to your square knots with loose knots

Cut of any extra hemp (Make your ends even).

Congratulations you now know two different kinds of knots you can use for hemp jewelry making. Let's learn a third type of knot, the twist knot, in the next chapter.

Chapter 4: Twist Knotting - How to make the twist macramé knot

We have learned how to make the square knot, placing a bead, and how to make loose square knots. I would like to show you how you can make another new knot, the twist macramé knot. Sounds fancy, huh? Well it's really is fancy but it really is not that hard to learn. It's great when something is easy to learn, isn't it? If you have read these chapters in order, then congratulations, you already know how to do this twist knot. In fact, you have already been practicing it. You may be really confused right now, scratching your head, going huh? Let's get starting on the knotting already so you can see what I mean.

I am going to jump ahead. You should already have a piece of jewelry started, whether it is going to be a necklace, bracelet, or anklet, that is up to you to decide. The twist knot is probably my favorite knot. I make the majority of my jewelry using the twist knot or some combination of it (Yes, you can do combinations of knots).

Loop the right long string over the middle strings.

Loop the left long string over the right long string.

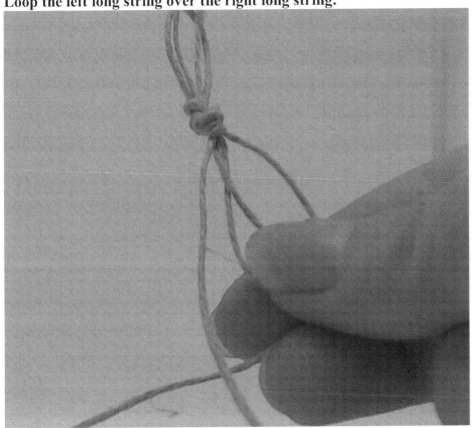

Now take that left long string under the right long string, and pull it through the big loop.

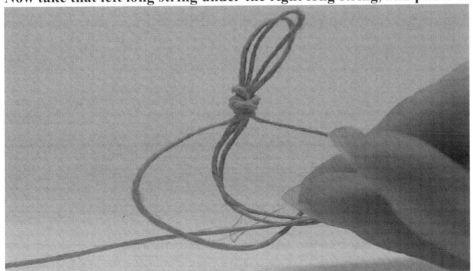

Pull your knot tight.

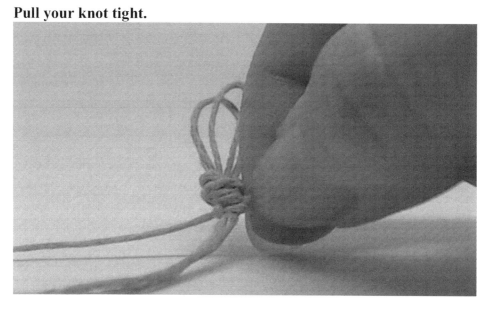

Repeat. Loop the right long string over the middle strings.
(Yes, the right long string, again!)

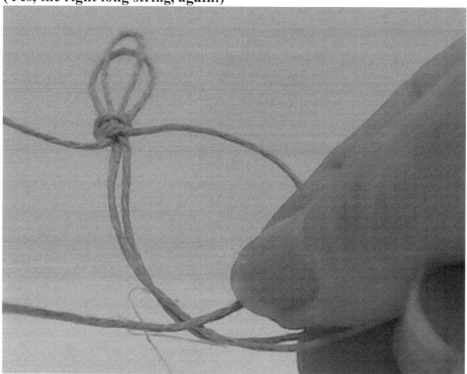

Loop the left long string over the right long string.

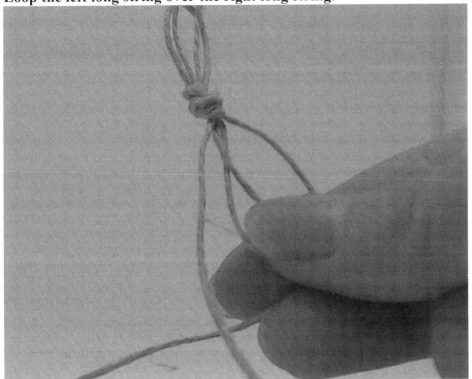

Now under the right long string, and pull it through again.

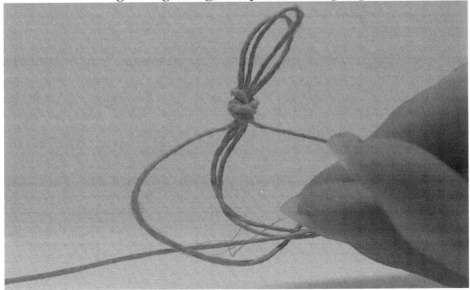

Pull your knot tight, again. After repeating a few times your twist knot jewelry should start to have a shape or pattern to it.

You may notice that your strings and jewelry piece are starting to twist. That is great, this is the twist knot after all! The string that was once on the left side is now on the right side. Twist your jewelry around until you find the string on the right side again. Don't worry if you get it mixed up a few times, your jewelry will still come out looking fine as long as you go back every now and then and make sure you have the right string on the right side. Continue to do this pattern for as long as you like.

You can mix in square knots too.

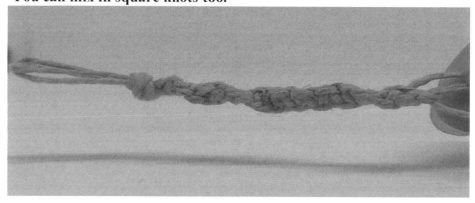

When place a bead on a twist knot jewelry piece, you have a couple of options. You can weave it in by placing the middle strings through the bead. Square knots will work best to hold the bead in place. You might like to place the bead on an outside string for a twist knot jewelry piece. This will make the bead appear to hang from your jewelry.

Chapter 4: Continued - Twist Knotting - How to make the twist macramé knot

Bead on a twist knot jewelry piece using the middle strings and square knots to hold in place.

Placing Bead on Twist Knot Hemp Jewelry - Step 1

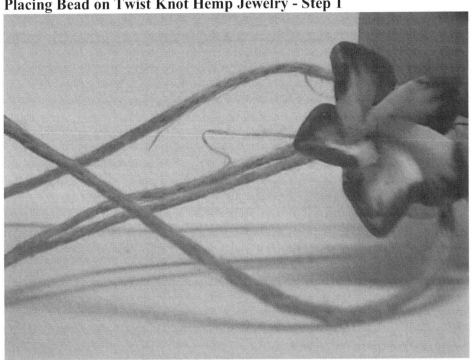

Placing Bead on Twist Knot Hemp Jewelry - Step 2

Placing Bead on Twist Knot Hemp Jewelry - Step 3

Placing Bead on Twist Knot Hemp Jewelry - Step 4

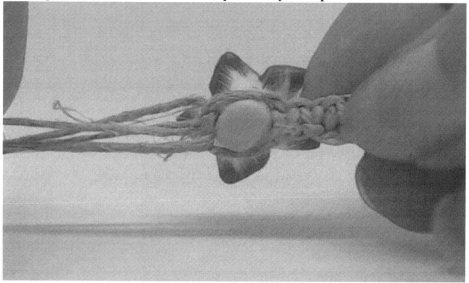

Bead on a twist knot jewelry piece using an outside long string and twist knots to hold the bead in place. (The longer your bead is in length, the more of a hanging affect your bead will have if you choose to thread it on a longer outside string versus the short middle strings).

Placing the bead on twist knot using the long string - Step One

Placing the bead on twist knot using the long string - Step Two

Placing the bead on twist knot using the long string - Step Three

Placing the bead on twist knot using the long string - Step Four

Finish your jewelry with an overhand knot.

Decide how much room you want to leave for adjusting your hemp jewelry piece.

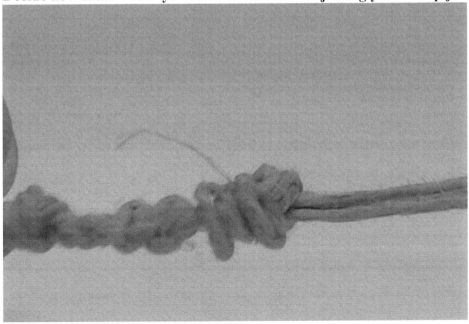

Tie another overhand knot.

Finished end of a hemp jewelry piece.

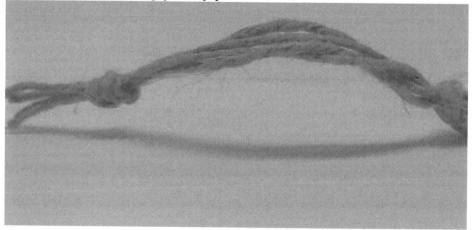

Cut the ends even with scissors.

That's three knots you now have. Can you imagine all the different possibilities of hemp jewelry with just those knots alone? Would you like to learn a couple more knots? Continue to chapter five to learn how to make the loose twist knot macramé.

Chapter 5: Loose Twist Knotting - Adding character to your twist knot with loose knotting

By now, you have learned how to do square knots, loose knots, and twist knots. Let's continue down this path of knotting and learn the loose twist macramé knot.

Start with a loop end that is made with an overhand knot. (See chapter one.)

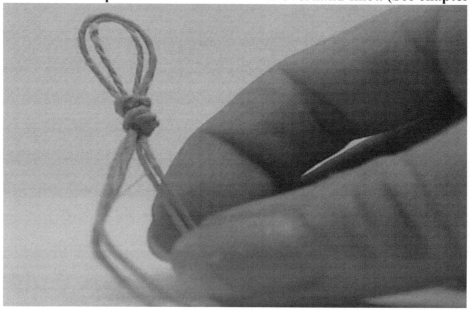

Loop the right long string over the middle short strings.

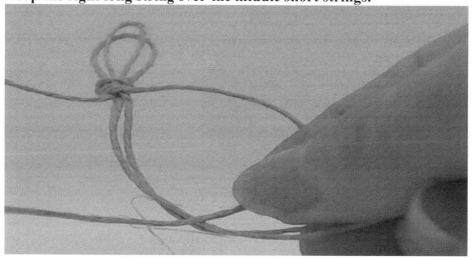

Chapter 5: Continued - Loose Twist Knotting - Adding character to your twist knot with loose knotting

Loop the left long string over the right long string.

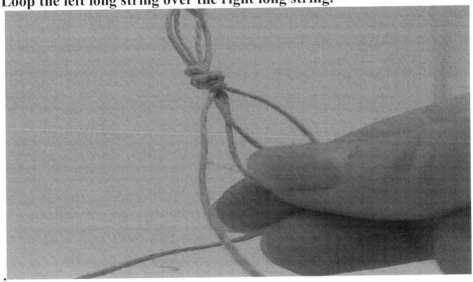

Now loop that same left string under all the strings.

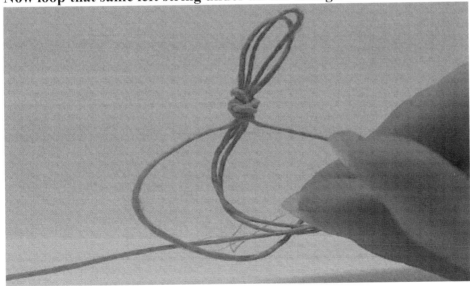

Pull the left long string through the big loop but not all the way. (You can decide here how loose you want your *loose twist knot* to be.)

(Here is a tip I haven't mentioned before. You might want to mix a tight knot after a loose knot to help your loose knot(s) stay in place, that is up to you. * But to maintain the twist pattern be sure to use a tight twist knot and stay on the same side to keep the flow smooth.)

To do a loose knot twist, you just keep repeating one side over and over. For example, the right side loose twist knot would look like the following photos.

Chapter 5: Continued - Loose Twist Knotting - Adding character to your twist knot with loose knotting

Looping the right long string over the middle short strings.

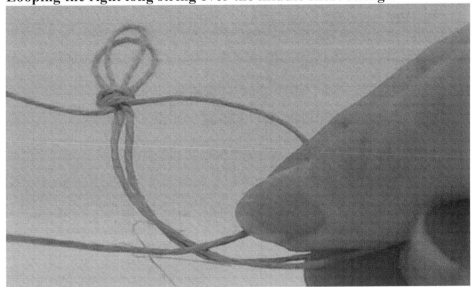

Looping the left long string over the right long string.

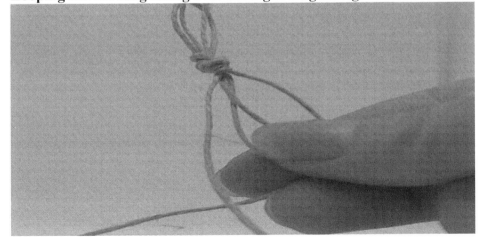

Looping the left long string under all the strings.

Pulling the left long string through the big loop, don't pull it too tight!

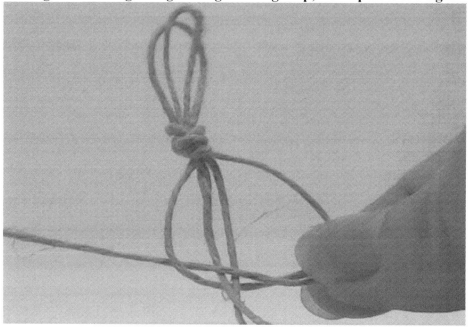

Chapter 5: Continued - Loose Twist Knotting - Adding character to your twist knot with loose knotting

Keep repeating. After a bit it will start to twist and look like this.

Decide if you want a bead on your loose twist knot macramé jewelry piece. Remember that tight square knots will hold your bead in place best. String your bead either on the middle short strings or on one of the outside strings. Make a couple tight square knots to secure your bead in place. Then you can continue with your loose twist knotting. You can see how interesting our jewelry is starting to turn out.

Finish your jewelry with an overhand knot.

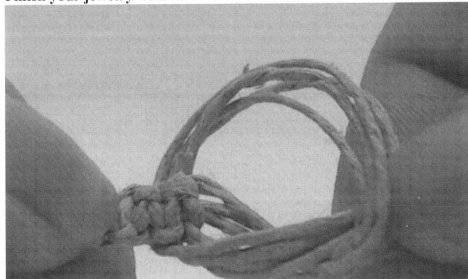

Decide how much room you want to leave for adjusting your hemp jewelry and tie another overhand knot.

Cut the ends even with scissors.

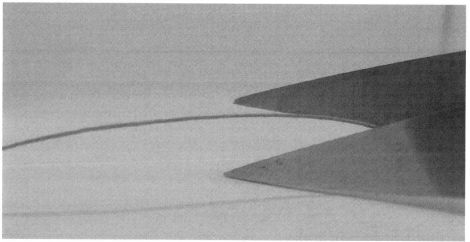

Great, now you have learned four different types of knots. Those are the knots I use for my beach hemp jewelry. You might want to learn how to braid with four strings. Let's continue on to the next chapter to see how braiding can be incorporated into your hemp jewelry.

Chapter 6: Braiding - Four String Braiding for Hemp Jewelry Making

I would like to show you just how good your jewelry pieces can look by mixing in some twist knotting and four-string braiding. If you have never done four-string braiding before, it can be a bit different at first. First decide if you want to make your jewelry piece completely out of braids or if you would like to try a mix of braids and knots. I say try them all and see what you like best. If you are going to make your entire piece out of braiding alone, you will need to use a different technique to start your jewelry pieces. You will want to measure out all your pieces the same length. Remember back in chapter one when we learned about measuring the length of your piece? The anklet that I wanted to make adjustable 8-12 inches longs, we ended up cutting our hemp string at thirty-two inches. For four-string braided only jewelry pieces you want all the pieces to be the same length. Let's do a little bit of quick math. We were at 12 inches and then I said let's add four extra inches to our string for a total of sixteen (refer back to chapter one). Take sixteen and multiply it by two. You get thirty-two inches. Let's measure out two pieces of string that are the same length ex. Thirty-two inches long for the hemp anklet mentioned above.

You will still start the piece just like we have started all of the other jewelry pieces with an overhand knot and loop to fasten. (See chapter one to review how to make the overhand knot.)

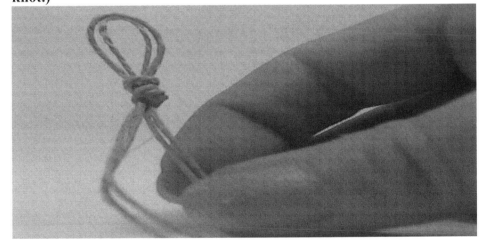

Chapter 6: Continued - Braiding - Four String Braiding for Hemp Jewelry Making

Whether you are mixing your braiding in with some knotting for your hemp jewelry piece or not, you will use all four of your strings in braiding. Let's look again at our four-strings picture.

Four Strings for Hemp Jewelry Making

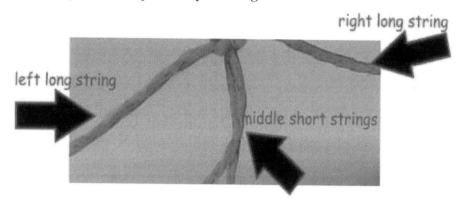

Right outer string goes over middle right string.

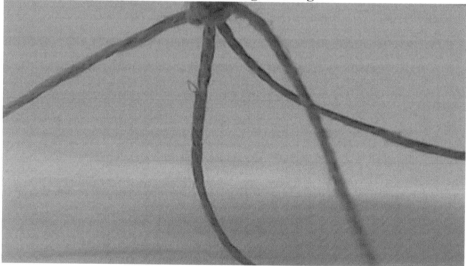

The same string then goes under the next string.

Finally take that string and it goes over the last string.

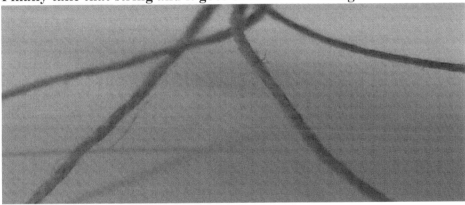

There will always be a new furthest right string that travels in this pattern over all the other strings. Remember to go in this order when braiding the strings: over, under, over, repeat. Continue to do this until you are satisfied with the amount of braiding.

After a while your jewelry piece will look like this.

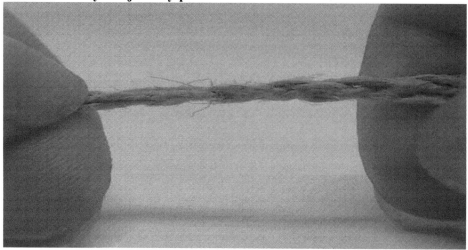

You might want to place a bead on your braided hemp jewelry piece.

Use an overhand knot to stop the braiding pattern.

Slide the bead on the middle strings or the outside string like I am doing here.

Tie another overhand knot.

Continue with your braiding or knotting.

To finish your braided hemp jewelry, you want to use another overhand knot.

Decide how much you want your jewelry to be adjustable.

Tie another overhand knot.

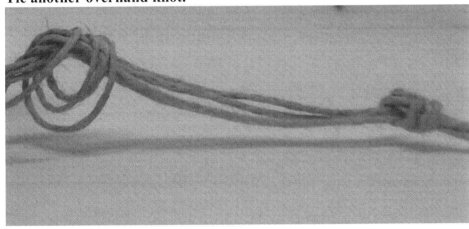

Cut off the ends even.

Your jewelry looks beautiful. I hope you had fun making it. If you need any more tips, continue to the next chapter for my online additional resources.

Chapter 7: Additional Resources - Links to my self-help YouTube videos

Making hemp jewelry is one of my favorite pass times. I have been making hemp jewelry and friendship bracelets since I was well a little girl, about twenty years now. One thing that I love is discovering new ways to do homespun projects at home. I guess you could say I am a geek about anything that has to do with jewelry making and hemp. YouTube has proved to be a valuable resource when I need information and I would like to share additional information for you on there as well.

Here are a few self-help links to my videos on YouTube:

https://www.youtube.com/watch?v=FKNdfr9I9XE

https://www.youtube.com/watch?v=sbLejefWpao

https://www.youtube.com/watch?v=yCxBKU_Xs8Y

https://www.youtube.com/watch?v=FKNdfr9I9XE&list=PLnLpws1arm8ah5SxJ7IRCqn5RN1-Wafya

That's the end of this book on hemp jewelry making. I hope you have learned a lot and enjoyed your time. You can really get lost in the knots and enjoy creating a million different combinations of hemp inspired jewelry.

Chapter 8: Glossary of Terms - The ABC's of terms I use to make my beach hemp jewelry

All natural - hemp made of 100% all-natural hemp no dye, no cord, just hemp

Braiding - a style of jewelry making where you move pieces of string over and under one another to make a pattern

Cord - hemp that has been dyed

Design - to create your own way of knotting or jewelry pieces

Exact - when measuring be sure to get the right measurement, be exact and precise

Freedom - you choose how you want to tie your knots, loose, tight, square, twist, braid, or a mixture of two or all of them!

Gather - getting together everything you think you could possibly need before you start your project

Hemp - the type of string that is use to make hemp jewelry, 100% all-natural hemp is brown in color.

Invent - create your own jewelry and style of knots by deciding how tight or loose you will make your knots

Jewelry - what we are making here

Chapter 8: Continued - Glossary of Terms - The ABC's of terms I use to make my beach hemp jewelry

<u>Knotting</u> - making a series of knots

<u>Looping</u> - laying one string over another string to make a hole or loop

<u>Macramé</u> - the style of knotting we are learning

<u>Necklaces</u> - one type of jewelry piece you could create out of hemp. You can make many other things out of hemp. I also make bracelets and anklets personally.

<u>Open</u> - remember to leave your starter loops open enough to thread an overhand knot through it so you can fasten your jewelry onto you or your friends and family

<u>Practice</u> - what it takes to get better at jewelry making!

<u>Quiet</u> - the sound you hear when you are making your hemp jewelry

<u>Right</u> - make sure you know your right from left before beginning to learn to make jewelry (Or anything really)

<u>Simple</u> - that is what I am going to keep this craft and lesson, simple

<u>Twist</u> - when the knot starts to form a spiral shape or curl around

<u>Umbrella</u> - you might need one at the beach if you make your jewelry there like me for protection from the rain or sun

<u>Variations</u> - by mixing knot types and using loose knots you can make a million different kinds of hemp jewelry patterns

<u>Wrap</u> - another name for the type of jewelry I make because it is wrapped around the body part it is worn on

<u>Xenia</u> - the Greek concept of hospitality; with hemp you can show others you care by making them a friendship necklace or bracelet

<u>Zephyr</u> - Anything of fine, light quality ex. Hemp

Made in the USA
Middletown, DE
15 July 2021